The Adventures of Padma and a Blue Dinosaur

VAISHALI SHROFF

Illustrated by
SUVIDHA MISTRY

For Non-Fiction, Turn to Page 55

HarperCollins *Children's Books*

First published in India in 2018 by HarperCollins Children's Books
An imprint of HarperCollins *Publishers*
A-75, Sector 57, Noida, Uttar Pradesh 201301, India
www.harpercollins.co.in

2 4 6 8 10 9 7 5 3 1
Copyright © Vaishali Shroff 2018
Illustrations © HarperCollins *Publishers* India

P-ISBN: 978-93-5277-743-3

Typeset in Libre Baskerville by Mukesh Kumar Aggarwal

Printed and bound at
Nutech Print Services - India

Introduction

If you are reading this, you must like dinosaurs a lot. When we learned about a fossil site in India, we were thrilled! We could now see the fossilized bones of dinosaurs that were discovered in our very own country. The next thing we knew, we were driving to the site at Rahioli, in the Kheda district of Gujarat, about 70 km from Ahmedabad.

Guess what happened there? After seeing the dinosaur fossil bones and eggs, I fell in love with them!

The experience at the fossil site was overwhelming. That evening, as we drove away from the fossil graveyard, a story took germ in my head. Characters were born. An adventure churned inside me like a whirlwind. That marked the beginning of *The Adventures of Padma and a Blue Dinosaur*.

The characters—Padma, her super grandma Labhuben, Rock Uncle and the baby dinosaur Bluethingosaurus—take us on a delightful adventure along River Narmada, a fossil-rich belt in central India. Following this story, we have an insightful section titled, 'All About Indian Dinosaurs'. It talks about India's dinosaur era, the people who are responsible for putting India on the world map of Palaeontology, and the most significant discoveries we have made thus far.

Like many of you, we have a huge pile of dinosaur books at home. But none of them talk about dinosaurs that were discovered in the Indian subcontinent. Who were these dinosaurs? Who discovered them and where? What were their names? Who did they prey on? How are dinosaur fossils excavated? Did we also discover dinosaurs similar to the very ferocious *Tyrannosaurus Rex* or the gigantic *Argentinosaurus* or the very small *Archeopteryx*?

And, of course, the most important question of them all: Can I be a Palaeontologist too?

This book aims to answer all these questions and much, much more!

So, if you love adventure and dinosaurs, hop aboard and let your fascinating adventure with Padma and Bluethingosaurus begin.

Foreword

It is indeed my pleasure to write the Foreword to this delightful story of Padma, the inquisitive little girl who, with her grandmother, manages cattle in the flatlands near Rahioli. Her life changes when Rock Uncle, the well-known Palaeontologist Professor Rajan Dinkar, gifts her a dinosaur egg. We are all set for high drama soon after, as the landscape transforms itself from fields and barren land to a hot and sweaty tropical jungle. You're truly in for a wonderful adventure, my friends!

Vaishali writes—with great knowledge and competence—a story of a remarkable adventure that traverses the rocky terrain of central India along the fossil-rich sedimentary belt of the amazing River Narmada. It is a story that both entertains and informs the readers.

The seven chapters of the story will grip the attention of all those who love dinosaurs and a fantastical world that is no more. Following the story, Vaishali introduces children to a world that existed nearly 66 million years ago, recounting how dinosaurs occupied the major supercontinent of Gondwanaland, of which India was a part. The major dinosaur taxa ranging from the Triassic to the Cretaceous periods are described in a way that children will love and understand.

Dinosaur studies in India have received a boost in the last 30 years, ever since scientists realized that these prehistoric creatures form a unique assemblage related to forms known from South America and Madagascar. They lived at a time when the Deccan volcanic eruptions were taking place and survived as well as they could. Several institutions have contributed to this study – primarily the Geological Survey of India, which found many new localities and genera. The Geological Studies Unit of the Indian Statistical Institute, Kolkata was the first to mount the skeleton of the giant sauropod, *Barapasaurus tagorei*. Universities and institutes have also significantly contributed to the study of dinosaur eggs and nests. The contents of their dung (coprolite) indicate the dinosaur's diet and the environment in which they lived.

Books like *The Adventures of Padma and a Blue Dinosaur* are rare and are needed to fire the imagination of young children who thirst for knowledge about the natural history of their own country. What better way can there be to quench the desire of voracious young readers who crave for knowledge, than a story that leads them to dream about a magical time that will never return?

My personal experience with young children—spanning several decades—has always left me amazed at the knowledge that young folk acquire in various ways. A young teenager once brought to my notice a mistake I had made in one of the panels while setting up a 'Dinosaurs of India' gallery at the Government Museum at Chandigarh. That moment was my biggest award – and I treasure it. I am sure that with books like this, storytelling with the message of learning will get its rightful place in the world of fiction.

Ashok Sahni
Lucknow
14 September 2017

Professor Ashok Sahni is currently Professor Emeritus at Panjab University. He obtained his Ph.D. in Geology from the University of Minnesota, Minneapolis, USA in 1968 and returned to India to work in the University of Lucknow and Chandigarh University. He is a Fellow/Associate at several prestigious scientific academies and societies, including the Third World Academy at Trieste, Italy; Humboldt Foundation, Germany; Associe Etranger Geol. Soc. France, Paris; Hon. MSVP, USA; and the Indian Science Academies. He has been associated with several UNESCO-IGCP projects as a national and international leader. He has worked at the American Museum of Natural History, New York; National Museum of Natural History, Washington DC; and has taught as a visiting Professor at Bonn University, Germany.

Currently, he is consultant to the Evolution Park and Gallery at Science City, Kapurthala. In 2011, he was awarded the prestigious Lifetime Achievement National Geoscience Award (2009) by the Government of India.

'For my grandmothers, Late Mrs Padmaben Kothari
and Mrs Labhuben Shah, the unsung heroes in my life.
For Arinjay and Vivikt, who are a constant inspiration.'

THE ADVENTURES OF PADMA AND A BLUE DINOSAUR

Dinosaur trail along the Narmada

The Girl Who Liked Adventures

Nothing changed, yet every day was different. As Padma stepped out of her school that afternoon and saw her grandmother, Labhuben, waiting in the distance, she wondered what adventures lay ahead.

As they moved towards the village, the herd of cows swayed in uniform motion. The sound of the bells tied around their necks was like many wind chimes tinkling together. Even the monkeys sitting on the trees along the road waited for them to pass by.

The cows seemed to be in no rush to get anywhere. But Labhuben was.

'Harrrrrrrrrrrrrrrrrrrrrrrr Chk Chk Harrrrrrrrrrrrrrrrrr!'

Labhuben's sharp voice could be heard clearly above the herd's orchestra. She earned a living by taking care of the cattle that toiled in a neighbour's cotton field in the village of Rahioli, in the Kheda district of Gujarat. After Padma's parents died in a famine several years ago, Labhuben was all Padma had. They lived in a small ancestral house that overlooked the fields of fluffy white cotton clouds.

Even after a long and hard day's work at the field, Labhuben's frail body never looked weary. She was well into her 70s, but she steered the cows with the agility of a young shepherd. Dressed in pastel shades of bandhani, with silver hoops in her drooping earlobes, she would hum a local folk song as she led the herd to a nearby flatland for grazing.

The herd always stopped before a 13th-century stone temple. The carvings on its walls had gathered moss over the years. The weather-beaten statues of the various gods and creatures seemed to be merging into one another as they told the story of a bygone era.

Labhuben removed her chappals, joined her hands and bowed to the Lord as she stood by the temple entrance; she did not enter the temple because it was dark. She knew that intricate cobwebs guarded its entrance, and it would break her heart to destroy a spider's work of art and labour.

'Oye, Gopi, wait! Wait na, Beenu! O, Baa, please wait!' Padma called out. Holding the straps of the khaki school bag that hung low on her back, she ran to catch up with Labhuben and her cows. Her plaits—coiled up in concentric circles and tied together with a red ribbon—flew behind her in the wind. Stopping only to catch her breath and pick up the sandal that had come off as she ran, she finally reached her grandmother.

Padma looked forward to this part of the day with her beloved grandmother, Labhuben, whom she fondly called 'Baa'. While Labhuben led the herd, Padma kept an eye on them. She loved the whistling sound of the breeze as it ruffled the leaves of the badam trees that lined the street, and the tinkling sound that came from a herd of happy cows.

When they reached the vast flatland, the cows munched their way into the tall grass, while Labhuben kept a watchful eye on them and Padma. Big and small rocks were scattered all over the place like confetti. Padma liked to sit by the large rocks and collect stones. Sometimes, she would make a stone tower. At other times, she would collect unusual stones and tie them into a knot at the end of her school uniform's dupatta. She would then put them in an old pickle jar at home, which she used as a treasure box.

Padma was fascinated by the engravings on the rocks. The engraved patterns looked like parts of animals to her – limbs, heads, tails, jaws, sharp teeth and even claws. Padma tried to complete the animal forms with a piece of chalk that she had in her school bag. The animals she drew looked like magical creatures that no one had ever seen – a cow-head with sharp teeth and the body of a giant bird, an elephant-head with the body of a snake, a giant fish with legs and a pair of wings, and a magnificent lizard with a lion's mane!

'Padu, your creatures resemble the mythical makaras!' exclaimed Labhuben, who loved to watch Padma draw across the rocks. 'Just like the ones carved on the old temple walls near our house!'

'Makaras?' said a bewildered Padma. 'I've never heard that word before.'

'In the epics of the Ramayana and Mahabharata, the makaras were referred to as strange, dragon-like sea monsters that looked like many animals put together. A makara was also the vahana of Goddess Ganga and of Lord Varuna. Goddess Ganga's makara had the head of an elephant, the body of a crocodile and the tail of a fish!' replied Labhuben.

'That must have been a difficult vehicle for Goddess Ganga to ride!' joked Padma. 'But did the makaras really exist?'

'We can never know. Maybe they did. They are carved along with deer, parrots and lions on the temple wall. So perhaps someone did see them along with the other familiar animals!' replied Labhuben. 'If Indra rode Airavat, an elephant with five heads; and Lord Vishnu rested on the thousand-headed serpent, Adishesha; and if our world has giant crocodiles and lizards, animals with big horns sticking out of their bodies – why not a makara?'

Padma smiled at her wise Baa and continued to draw more makaras.

The Rare Discovery

It tumbled. But she built it again. Padma's stone tower was the tallest she had ever made!

Soon, the air at the flatland was filled with the sound of hammering and chiselling of rocks, and the gentle tremors made Padma's stone tower tumble all over again.

Padma turned around, and there he was.

'Rock Uncle!' Padma called out.

It was professor Rajan Dinkar – Rock Uncle, as Padma fondly called him. When he was not teaching biology at the local college, he was seen at the flatland, examining certain rocks. He worked as an assistant with senior palaeontologists and geologists at the Ahmedabad branch of the Geological Survey of India (GSI).

With a hat on his head and a tool bag tied across his waist, he would move among the rocks, examining each of them carefully. He would begin by dusting off the rocks with a big brush, then tap them gently with his knuckles— sometimes even planting his ear close to the surface to listen to any sounds—and chip at them with a small chisel.

'What are you looking for in the rocks?' asked Padma.

'Sshhhh! There are little secrets waiting to be told,' he said, with a hint of mystery in his voice. 'I'm trying to discover mysterious dinosaur fossils and learn some more secrets!'

'Dino-what-did-you-say?' Padma asked, crinkling her forehead and leaning forward, her large, almond-shaped eyes wide open with curiosity.

'They are called "die-no-sore fos-sils",' replied Rock Uncle. 'Dinosaurs were gigantic creatures that lived on our planet more than 66 million years ago. While there are many theories, it is believed that meteors and asteroids crashed into the Earth's surface, which snowballed into various earthquakes, tsunamis, volcanic

eruptions and other natural calamities across the globe. Boom! In an instant, almost all plant and animal life, including the dinosaur race, was completely wiped out!'

Rock Uncle continued, 'The bones in our body do not contain many minerals that bacteria can eat. That's why they don't decompose. What you see on the rocks are bones from the various body parts of dinosaurs that got buried here after they died. They are called fossils, and this flatland is known as a fossil graveyard. Palaeontologists like me are still trying to find out more about these mysterious animals. Like this one here is the fossilized skull of a *Rajasaurus narmadensis*. And this is the thigh bone and joint of a *Titanosaurus indicus*. And ...'

Padma could not believe what she had just heard. And the dinosaurs had names too! She pointed to the creatures she had drawn on the rocks. 'Then here is my Cowasaurus. And this is my Haathisaaposaurus. And those that I've drawn there

are my Flyingfishosaurus and Lionosaurus. You know, once Lionosaurus attacked poor Cowasaurus and Haathisaaposaurus came to save her. And then ...' Padma's stories were endless.

'You are my little palaeontologist!' said Rock Uncle as he took his hat off and put it on Padma's head, much to her delight.

'Dinkarbhai, the old temple outside has carvings of animals like the one Padma has drawn on the rocks. They were called makaras in our Vedas and Puranas. Are they the same as dinosaurs?' Labhuben asked. 'If that's the case, then it's strange to even imagine that the makaras I've been bowing to every day, all these years, are buried right here, in this very flatland!'

'Hmmm ... maybe the makaras are known as dinosaurs in English,' said Padma, as she laughed and high-fived her Baa.

Each day spent with Rock Uncle was a journey into the prehistoric world for Padma. He would show her pictures of dinosaurs from various books and tell her more about their life and times. She would even take some books home to read. Padma was careful not to draw on the rocks as those mysterious shapes could be an important fossil and Rock Uncle would need to study them. She even became wary of stepping on rocks around the flatland – what if they had fossils embedded in them?

'Time to head back, Padu!' Labhuben called out. She did not know how to read or write, but she could tell the exact time of the day looking at the sky.

As they were walking back to gather the cows, Padma stumbled upon a rock that was nestled in a bed of grass. It had circles all over it.

'Rock Uncle! Please come here! Look at this rock. It's unlike anything I've ever seen before!' Padma called out anxiously.

Rock Uncle hurried to

the spot. As he stood by Padma and Labhuben, staring at the rock, his eyes slowly widened and his jaw dropped; his chisel slid off his hands and fell to the ground.

'Eggs! You've discovered a whole nest of dinosaur eggs! This is no ordinary rock, Padma,' Rock Uncle exclaimed excitedly.

Padma could not believe that there was a whole nest of eggs embedded in that rock. Eggs that could tell a lot about what had happened tens of millions of years ago. Padma had joined the elite list of people who had discovered dinosaur eggs! She beamed as Labhuben put her arms around her shoulders.

'I'd love to hold a dinosaur egg! I've only seen it in books,' Padma said.

Rock Uncle hurried back to where he had kept his bag. He opened an old metal suitcase with rusty hinges and held out a grey-coloured oval stone.

'Keep this dinosaur egg. I discovered many eggs last month, but this one is special,' Rock Uncle said as he gently handed it over to Padma.

'Wow! Is that really for me? Thank you, Rock Uncle! This is so precious!' Padma said, unable to believe that she was holding an actual dinosaur egg in her hands.

'It's precious indeed. Generally, eggs are found in clusters. When I discovered this egg, it was the only one in the pit. It was surrounded by the fossilized bones of a carnivorous dinosaur,' explained Rock Uncle.

'It could have survived an attack! It really is special,' said Padma, hugging the egg.

'Harrrrrrrrrrrrrrrrrr chk chk haarrrrrrrrrrr,' Labhuben called out to her cows. 'Padma, looks like your scary animals are going to jump right out of the rocks and pounce on my poor cows. We better hurry before it gets too dark,' said Labhuben as she started to usher the herd out of the flatland.

The sun was setting and the sky had turned a beautiful shade of vermillion. Labhuben and Padma smiled as they waved goodbye to Rock Uncle. Padma held the dinosaur egg very carefully in her hands. This was one egg she could not afford to break.

As Padma and her grandmother walked away, the tinkling of the cow bells slowly faded into the night, and Padma's mysterious makaras sat quietly on the rocks, staring at the stars in the darkening sky.

A Whole New World

'**G**o to sleep now. You've had a long day,' Labhuben said to her cows as she tethered them in a shed outside the house. It was bedtime for everyone. But Padma could not sleep. She wouldn't let Labhuben sleep either.

'Baa, what if the dinosaur baby is still inside the egg? Do you think it could hatch? What if it's an ancestor ... you know?' Padma asked. 'Rock Uncle once told me that we have evolved from other beings.'

'I have a feeling it's a makara!' said Labhuben as she touched the egg, her wrinkly skin looking like the pattern on the egg.

'No, no. I'm sure it's a dinosaur. What if

the egg hatches and out comes a genie to grant our wishes!' Padma continued hopefully. 'What if it's a dinosaur genie!'

'What if it's a makara genie!' added Labhuben dreamily.

'Maybe a flying dinosaur genie that will take us places as we sit on its back!' said Padma.

'We may need a really tall ladder to get on its back though,' said Labhuben.

'Or we could just hang on its neck like it's the trunk of an elephant!' said Padma. Her imagination had taken full flight.

Padma ran her hands along the stone-like egg. *Where do I keep it? It can't break. It shouldn't break.* Padma's eyes fell on her pickle jar where she kept her stones. She emptied the pickle jar, carefully placed the egg inside it and put the lid back on firmly. She then put the jar on a shelf near the window of the room in which she and Labhuben slept every night.

As Padma settled down for the night on the colourful patchwork mattress that Labhuben had handcrafted from her old saris, she could see the moon through the window shining brightly. It was Poornima, a full-moon night. She could even see the crater formations on the moon's pearly white surface. It almost seemed to be keeping guard, its light falling directly on the dinosaur egg, much like a spotlight. It was an unusual sight, but Padma's head was brimming with questions about the egg, so she didn't give it a second thought.

Padma couldn't take her eyes off the jar. As she lay next to her grandmother, getting ready to sleep, she asked, 'Baa, of all the dinosaurs that Rock Uncle has told me about, I wonder which one this egg belongs to. What if it's not a dinosaur egg at all, but an ostrich egg? I've read in my books that they have one of the largest eggs in the world and that birds have evolved from dinosaurs!'

'Go to bed now. It's late!' said Labhuben, patting Padma, gently urging her to sleep.

The next morning, a panic-stricken Padma woke Labhuben up. 'The egg! Where is the egg? Where is the jar? I don't see it anywhere!' She looked around and nothing was the same any more. Their house was gone! Even the air smelled peculiar. 'Where are we? Baa, where are we?'

Padma rubbed her eyes hard to wake herself up. Labhuben opened her wrinkled eyelids and tied her dishevelled hair.

'How could the egg just vanish? What happened after we fell asleep?' said a confused Labhuben.

'Maybe a bird entered the house when we were asleep and knocked the jar over. Maybe someone cast a magic spell on us! Or maybe a thief stole the precious egg. I am sure many people want to steal the wonderful fossils that Rock Uncle discovers.' Padma's mind was buzzing with possibilities.

'But where is the house!? I am sure the birds or thieves didn't carry the house with them!' said Labhuben as she looked all around her.

The mattress was gone. The walls and the roof were gone. They were sleeping on a bed of thick roots that extended out of tall, dense trees.

'You're right! Where is our house, Baa?!' It was all too weird and scary. Padma and Baa huddled together. Then they saw something familiar covered with leaves. Padma lifted the leaves with trembling hands, and there it was. 'The jar! The egg!' screamed Padma. Enveloped by long leaves, the jar with the egg seemed absolutely unaffected by the changes.

'I am so glad nothing has happened to my precious egg. What would I tell Rock Uncle?' said a relieved Padma. She picked up the jar and held it against her chest.

'But it makes me wonder – how come everything has vanished but this egg?' said Labhuben and tapped her chin thoughtfully.

Just then, they heard a strange sound ...

'UMMMMMMMMMMMM UMMMMMMMMMOOOOOOOOOOOOOOOOOO!'

Padma felt a nudge on her neck and a strong gust of wind, like someone had just thrust her before a pedestal fan running at full speed. She was scared to turn around. And when she did, what she saw seemed straight out of a fairy tale. For it's not every day that you see a strange-looking creature stick its head out from between trees and stare back at you. A strange, blue creature with a very small head and a long, unending neck.

'Snake! Snake! Baaaaaa! Snake!' Padma screamed.

The long-necked blue creature nodded slowly and began to move forward from behind the trees.

'Padu, maybe it's a giraffe – look at the brick-like spots on its long neck!' said Labhuben.

'No, Baa! It can't be a giraffe. Its legs are too short and stodgy. Have you looked at its face closely?' asked Padma. 'It looks like a hyena. I've seen it in one of the books. It's exactly like that!'

'It has the face of a hyena and
the body of a giraffe. But its blue. Hey Bhagwan! What kind of creature is
this!' exclaimed a rather confused Baa.

'YUUUUUUUMEEEEEMUMMMMMMYYYYYYYY!'

It sounded like complete gibberish.

'What was that? Yuuuuuu-meeee-mummyyyyy?' Padma asked the blue
creature, craning her neck to look at his face. 'Me mummy? No. No way!
You're mistaken, you ... er ... blue ... er ... thing,' Padma replied, shocked at what
it was asking.

Mustering up some courage, Labhuben peeked behind the tree to see what the
blue thing looked like. Her eyes almost popped out of her head as she stood
staring at the creature. 'Padu! It's a makara. Just come and have a look at it!'

'No, Baa! This is definitely a dinosaur. I've seen pictures like these in Rock Uncle's
books. I wish he were here to explain to us!'

The village had transformed into a deep forest. Dense vegetation had replaced
the fields and farms. It seemed like the house had travelled overnight to a
different period, a different place.

Padma rubbed her eyes in disbelief. When she opened them again, she hoped to
see her village. But ... nothing changed.

'You me mummy? You me mummy?' the blue thing squealed with pleading eyes
as he looked at Padma and Labhuben.

'Padma, what should we call this blue thing? Surely, it needs a name!' said
Labhuben as the blue thing hovered around them, munching on tree leaves.

'Er ... right, Baa. Er ... Blue ... something ... saurus? Bluesaurus! Bluethingosaurus!'

'Aha! Bluethingosaurus – a long name, just like his long neck! And he is an
Isisaurus. One of the most peculiar looking sauropods to have been found in India.
He is like a giraffe with short legs. Bluethingosaurus, it is such an honour and
delight to see you in person!' said Rock Uncle, as he slowly approached the scene.

'Dinkarbhai! Thank goodness you are here. We don't know where we are. It's all
so strange,' said Labhuben, relieved and delighted to see Rock Uncle.

'Yes, it's very absurd. I woke up this morning and found myself in this deep
forest. Everything around me had disappeared, except my camera, which was still
hanging around my neck! And some tools in my pockets. You are the first people

I've met so far. I'm so glad to see you both!' said Rock Uncle.

Bluethingosaurus heard a new voice and turned around.

'You know me name! You me mummy? Ummmmoooooooooooo!!' said Bluethingosaurus.

'Sorry, but I'm not your mummy, Bluethingosaurus. I can try and help you find her though,' replied Rock Uncle.

'We must help him find his family,' said Padma.

'Yes, we must!' Labhuben added excitedly.

'I want me mummy!' said Bluethingosaurus.

As they were speaking, Rock Uncle noticed Padma holding the jar containing the egg. 'Isn't that the egg I gave you, Padma?' he asked, pointing to the jar.

'Yes! You know Uncle, it's so strange. This egg did not vanish with the other things. It stayed the way it was – in this jar,' replied Padma, still astonished.

'I told you. It's a special egg!' said Rock Uncle, smiling at her. He looked around, pondering their situation. 'We seem to have gone back in time by about 70 million years, to the late Cretaceous Period of the dinosaurs. The Mesozoic era. At this moment, we are perhaps the oldest humans!' said Rock Uncle.

'Older than the oldest mummy of Egypt!' Padma was enjoying this new adventure. 'Maybe this egg got us here!'

'Who knows!' said Labhuben, shrugging her shoulders.

'Yes, who knows!' added Rock Uncle.

Padma gave the jar to Rock Uncle so he could keep it safely in his bag.

Together, they walked into a new and mysterious world with a blue dinosaur following close behind.

The kingdom of Jabalpuriya

The camera oscillated like a pendulum around Rock Uncle's neck as he walked. His tools stuck out of his waist pouch. He couldn't stop taking pictures of the gorgeous foliage he was witnessing – a wonderful blend of various shades of green, blue, brown.

'I feel like an astronaut who takes pictures of outer space that no one else can see with their own eyes!' he said.

Padma and Labhuben marvelled at the beautiful landscape. Bluethingosaurus looked around, hoping to spot someone else who looked like him.

It was only when it started to get dark did they realize how much they had walked. Padma held her Baa gently as they walked. She was worried her grandma might stumble and fall as her old eyes could not see too well in the dark.

'Maybe we should just sit under this tree till the break of dawn. We don't know what creatures are lurking around to feast on us,' said Rock Uncle, as he cleaned his camera lens.

Labhuben nodded in agreement, and Padma collapsed by the trunk of the tree.

'Ummmmooooo!' said Bluethingosaurus. Then, he kneeled next to Padma and curled up to sleep. They were all so tired that they didn't notice the hooting and roaring sounds around them.

The next morning, when the sun was out, Bluethingosaurus was the first to wake up.

'Ummmm Ummmmm! Sniff sniff!' He nuzzled everyone till they were all awake, yawning and stretching before starting to walk again. A short while later, the forest cover cleared and they reached a vast expanse of land.

It was an unusual morning. There were no crowing roosters or chirping sparrows or melodious canaries. Instead, the air was filled with deep and raucous bellowing sounds like many cars honking together. The sky was clear and one could see the horizon.

Soon, they found themselves before a giant gold-coloured fortress with imposing gates. It was surrounded by thick vines and interlocked branches that made it almost inaccessible.

THHHHHHUUUUDDDDDDDDDDDDDDDDDDDDDD!

A loud sound like the thunderous thumping of footsteps made them stop in their tracks. Bluethingosaurus ducked behind Padma.

'What just happened? Whoaaaaaaaaaaaaaaaaaaaaaaaaaa!!!' gasped Padma in alarm.

As the dust settled, they saw before them two dinosaurs of giant proportions. Although they looked like Bluethingosaurus, they were still quite different. Everyone was stunned. They had only read about their sizes and seen them in pictures. But to see the large sauropods in person was intimidating, to say the least.

'Who are you? What are you doing in the Kingdom of Jabalpuriya? And who is that blue creature with you? We've never seen anyone quite like him in and around our kingdom.' Their raspy voice startled everyone.

'He's Bluethingosaurus. We are looking for his family,' said Padma innocently, as she patted him affectionately on his side, as if he was a dear pet.

Bluethingosaurus looked up at the two giants and said, 'You look me mummy!'

'What? No! We are not your mummies, and we must put you in our dungeons. We cannot take chances with potential enemies,' said one of the guards.

'No! No! We are not your enemies! We want to meet the King. We have an offer for him,' said Labhuben, trying to sound confident even as her legs trembled.

'Are you sure about what you just said, Baa? What offer are you talking about?' asked Padma curiously.

'I shall talk only to the King now,' said Labhuben firmly, crossing her arms across her chest and looking away.

'Okay then, let's go,' said one of the guards.

'Are you sure, Mahaan? What if they are imposters? How can we just allow them into our kingdom?' said the other guard.

'No, Baahu. Something tells me they aren't imposters. Let our King decide!' replied Mahaan as he pushed the gates open. The creaky sounds were deafening. But what they saw inside was mesmerizing. Hundreds of dinosaurs going as far into the distance as they could see.

'These are titanosaurian dinosaurs. They are sauropods. Can you believe that such large animals survive only on grass and leaves?' said Rock Uncle.

'Just like our majestic elephants who live only on greens and loads of bananas!' added Labhuben.

'Absolutely! And these short and woody palm-like trees that you see here are cycads. They are over 300 million years old and are no longer found abundantly in the world!' explained Rock Uncle.

'Aren't these fern trees, Rock Uncle? Didn't know they were so old too! If the cycads and ferns could talk and move like us, they would be one of the oldest living people on Earth!' said Padma. She was thrilled to be 70 million years back in time.

The two guards escorted them inside King Jabalpuriya's palace.

'Mahaan and Baahu, who have you brought to my court? They don't look like they belong in our land!' the King said.

'Your Highness! We found these strange-looking creatures snooping around our kingdom. They say they have some kind of offer for you,' said Baahu.

'Aaaaaaaaaaaaaaaacchhhooooooooooooooooo!!' The King sneezed. The stone murals moved. The floor trembled a little. Mahaan and Baahu did not move an inch. But Labhuben, Padma, and Rock Uncle were lifted off the ground and blown to one side of the court.

'Sorry about that. I have a minor cold. What offer are you talking about?' The King's voice was powerful, yet it had a hint of kindness.

'We can cook delicious vegetarian meals for you, Your Majesty. Food that you'd relish and never forget! Give us a chance, Your Majesty, to cook you the meal of your life in return for a favour. We need your help to find Bluethingosaurus's family. He needs his mummy,' Baa pleaded.

'I want me mummy! Paaaleeeez! Sniffff! Ummmoooooooooo!' cried Bluethingosaurus.

The King thought for a moment and said, 'I would love to try new dishes. You will get one day in our kitchen to cook. Show us what you can do, and we shall consider your request.'

After a detailed inspection of the ingredients in the kitchen—a variety of roots, leaves, stems, cassava, club mosses, nuts and fruits—Baa started to work like a machine. While Padma helped with the cutting and chopping, Rock Uncle stirred the food with huge wooden sticks in large, prehistoric saucepans made of rocks and stones. The food cooked on a woodfire. Turned out, Rock Uncle was not only a professor and a palaeontologist but also a good sous chef!

Soon, some humble root and stem curries spiced with herbs, fern fritters, a leafy salad and some rice-like grains made their way to the King's dining table. Labhuben, Rock Uncle and Padma stood on high chairs to see the King's reaction to the food.

The King lifted the giant bowl and went 'slurp' at the curry. Then he went 'slurp slurp slurp' and soon he went 'slurp slurp slurp slurp slurp slurp'! He turned the bowl upside down till the last drop of the curry trickled down into his open mouth. He finished off by licking his face with his long tongue!

The King chomped through the leafy salad and crunched on the crispy fritters. Once his meal was over, he stared into Padma's large eyes. Padma's slender legs shook with fear, but the look on the King's face told her that he had found the meal utterly delightful! She inched closer to Labhuben. Bluethingosaurus inched closer to Padma. Rock Uncle couldn't wait for the King's verdict.

'Mahaan and Baahu, the two best soldiers from my army, will join you on your expedition to find Bluethingosaurus's family. You will need them for protection against the wild ones,' said the King. 'Be careful. Those outside my kingdom may not be kind to you. Take this rock with you. My uncle, *Bruhathkayosaurus* from the kingdom of Kallamedu, had given it to me. It's very special – if you rub it, it lights up in the dark. You can see everything around you, but no one can see you. Keep it safe for it was handed down to my ancestors by their ancestors – *Barapasaurus tagorei* and *Kotasaurus yamanpalliensis* from the kingdom of Yamanapalli.'

Rock Uncle put the rock carefully in his sling bag along with the jar. Now his bag was precious indeed!

'Thank you, mighty King Jabalpuriya, for your generosity and for showing faith in us with this precious rock. We will take good care of it,' said Labhuben.

'Thaaaaaankyoooouuuuuuuuuu!' said Bluethingosaurus happily.

They were grateful to the King for his noble gesture. As the King marched back into his palace room, the four of them looked at each other – not knowing what to expect as they stepped out of the palace into the kingdom beyond.

Bhedaghat   Jabalpur

The Encounter at Bhedaghat

The silent and still waters of the Narmada looked like satin brushing against the mighty Amarkantak mountain range. The view along the river bank was breathtaking.

Bluethingosaurus looked all around like children look out of the window on their first bus ride. Everything was new, everything was strange. And yet, he didn't feel lonely.

While Padma and Labhuben sat on Bluethingosaurus's back, Rock Uncle sat on Mahaan's. Mahaan led the way, and Baahu brought up the rear to protect them from a stealthy attack.

'The world looks so different when I sit on your back, Bluethingo!' Padma said, as she looked around in wonder.

'It so naaaaaaaaice. Like youuuuuuuu! Ummmmmooooo!'

'When will you roar like the other dinosaurs?' Padma asked. 'I can't even imagine you roaring.'

'When I be bigggggg. Like Mahaan. Like Baaahu. I go RAAAWWWWWRRRRRR UMOOOOOOOOOOOO!'

Padma and Labhuben laughed at Bluethingosaurus's feeble attempts at roaring.

'If we don't find your mummy, don't worry! You have us as family!' Padma hugged Bluethingosaurus.

On the way, Mahaan and Baahu nodded at other friendly giant dinosaurs. They were all sauropods, like the *Jainosaurus* and *Titanosaurus*.

'Why are Mahaan and Baahu orange and Bluethingosaurus, er ... blue? Do all dinosaurs have a different skin colour?' asked Padma.

'It's very strange. You remember the fossil of a dinosaur skin I showed you at Rahioli? It's very difficult to determine their colour from a fossil. So we really didn't know that an *Isisaurus* was blue and a *Titanosaurus* was orange. But, it's wonderful to see so much colour, isn't it?' replied Rock Uncle.

Suddenly, Labhuben cautioned them. 'I think I saw someone behind that tree!'

'Stop! Stand back. We've got company!' Mahaan alerted everyone, for he, too, had heard rustling sounds from behind the trees. Something seemed to be running swiftly along the dried, fallen leaves.

A moment later, whatever was behind the tree stepped out and stood before them on two feet − staring up at them with piercing eyes. Their mouths, with razor-sharp teeth, were wide open, as though waiting to tear something apart. The team from Jabalpuriya was surrounded by hungry, vicious dinosaurs. Although these dinosaurs were much smaller in size, they did not seem intimidated by the enormous giants, Mahaan and Baahu.

'We have reached Bhedaghat, and these must be theropods − *Indosuchus* and *Laevisuchus*,' said Rock Uncle. 'They don't stand a chance against Mahaan and Baahu. You wait and watch how they fight!'

'Mahaan and Baahu don't look like they will fight or scare them away. Perhaps it's our last day together, Baa,' Padma said, nervously.

'The body soooooooo smaalllll. The teeeeeeth so biggggggg!' exclaimed Bluethingosaurus, as he moved back a bit.

Suddenly, the peaceful-looking Baahu roared loudly. Padma and Labhuben thought the sky would split.

STOMP! SWOOOOOOOOOOOOOOOOOOOSHHHHH!

A couple of the dinosaurs hung on Baahu's mighty legs. But Baahu stomped his feet and swished his mighty tail from side to side. The tail struck the ferocious lizards. Mahaan followed suit. Rock Uncle clung to Mahaan's back as he felt everything tremble.

'That *Indosuchus* has flown into oblivion! And look at that pack of bipedal *Laevisuchus*!' Rock Uncle was amazed to witness this glorious encounter – the sound of the tail striking out and the heavy stomping that shook the rocks and scared away many of the smaller dinosaurs.

'Watch out, Padma!' Rock Uncle screamed.

A *Laevisuchus* came charging towards Bluethingosaurus. Poor Bluethingosaurus froze. He was not as big as an adult *Isisaurus* yet, and he didn't look like he could let out a loud roar.

Padma had to do some quick thinking. She asked Bluethingosaurus to stand in front of Mahaan, so that as soon as the predator pounced, they could move out of the way. Bluethingosaurus followed Padma's instructions. The little wild predator found himself face to face with the enormous, looming figure of Mahaan. Another strike of his tail and the dinosaur pack receded into the forest.

'That was quick thinking, Padma!' said Rock Uncle as he clicked a
few pictures. His camera was a priceless weapon, for not only did
it capture pictures of the fight, but its flash also managed to scare
some dinosaurs away!

'We have a constant battle with these meat-eating animals, to
protect everyone who lives in this kingdom,' said a proud Mahaan.

The storm had passed. They proceeded on their journey with
the humble and noble giants of Jabalpuriya. At every bend, they
marvelled at the beauty of prehistoric life. Soon they reached
a misty waterfall.

'This is the most beautiful waterfall I've ever seen!' exclaimed Labhuben.

'I think these are the mystifying Dhuandhar falls that one can see in our world now. On both sides of the seaway are the amazing marble rocks. Can you imagine? These rocks contain the fossils of prehistoric life that we are seeing right now. Perhaps the fossils of *Titanosaurus, Jainosaurus, Indosaurus* and *Laevisuchus* that we have discovered in Rahioli could be of the same animals we have encountered on our journey!' said Rock Uncle.

'And could the *Titanosaurus* ones belong to Mahaan and Baahu?' enquired Padma.

'Most certainly, Padma! That's a possibility!' replied Rock Uncle.

They soaked in the beauty of the magical falls and of the pristine waters of the Narmada against the pure white marble rocks that looked like they had been neatly woven together and stacked in layers.

'Here, have these fruits. You must be hungry. We have been munching on leaves and grass all along the way,' said Baahu. He handed them a variety of pulpy fruit, nuts and leaves. They ate quickly, too hungry to think about what they were eating.

'Baahu, let's leave before it gets dark. We will be entering the territory of the mighty carnivores soon, and that's not good news,' said Mahaan.

'It's not going to be easy. Let's all be alert. Although being on guard may not be enough to save us,' said Baahu.

Once again, they were on their way. They did not fancy meeting the king of carnivores.

The Escape Plan

Padma fell asleep on Bluethingosaurus's back, her body swaying as they moved along. It had been a tiring journey. Labhuben held her tight lest she slid off his back.

Another day had gone by. Bluethingosaurus was losing hope. He wasn't sure if he would ever find his family. They decided to stop near a clump of trees to rest and were soon fast asleep, their snores mingling with the sounds of the wilderness in the dark.

'RAAAAWWWWWWWWWWWWWWWWWWWRRRRRRRR HUMPPHHHHHHUMPPHHHHH RRRAAAWWWWWWWWWRRRRRRRRRRR!!'

'What's that sound, Mahaan? I'm scared!' Padma hugged her Baa tight.

'We can't see anything,' replied Mahaan.

'The rock! The rock! Let's use the rock that King Jabalpuriya gave us,' said Rock Uncle. He carefully removed it from his bag and rubbed it. The rock started to glow and radiate a neon light.

As Rock Uncle moved the rock around to see where the sound was coming from, they saw several pairs of bright orange eyes looking in their direction from a distance. They were not as big as the *Titanosaurus*, but they were one of the wildest dinosaurs Rock Uncle had ever seen.

'That's the *Rajasaurus narmadensis*! Look at the little bump-like crest on its head. And we are probably close to home as the *Rajasaurus* was discovered in Gujarat too,' said Rock Uncle.

Padma was visibly excited. 'Wow! Our house could be somewhere close by. What

if we are standing right on our flatland!'

It was the *Rajasaurus* indeed. Though some fossils had been discovered in Jabalpur, they were mainly found in Rahioli.

'Ssshhhhhhhhhhh, Padma. They can't see us. But they can surely hear us or even smell us. Let's not give them a ready multi-course buffet to feast on, with Mahaan and Baahu for the main course. Did you know that the *Rajasaurus* and *Titanosaurus* fossil bones were discovered in the same pit in Rahioli? Which means that the *Rajasaurus* could easily prey on a gigantic *Titanosaurus*!' said Rock Uncle.

Sitting on the dinosaurs' backs, they debated the plan of action to evade the herd of *Rajasaurus*. A combat was out of the question.

'What if we make a quick dash across the seaway? To the other side?' Labhuben thought aloud.

'Baahu and I will not be able to match their speed. They will catch up with us in no time at all and tear us apart!' whispered Mahaan.

'What if we distract them by hurling stones or rocks into the river? And when they go to the river to check, we can escape!' Padma suggested.

'Clever plan, Padma! We can't be sure if it will work, but right now, it seems to be our only option to avoid getting killed,' said Baahu.

Rock Uncle moved the torch-like rock around and saw two *Rajasaurus*. They seemed to be

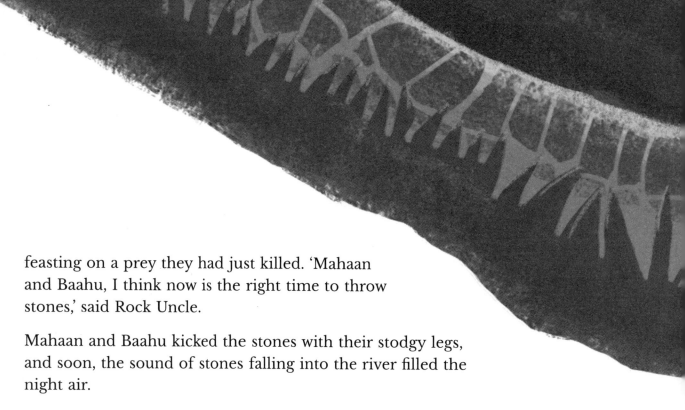

feasting on a prey they had just killed. 'Mahaan and Baahu, I think now is the right time to throw stones,' said Rock Uncle.

Mahaan and Baahu kicked the stones with their stodgy legs, and soon, the sound of stones falling into the river filled the night air.

'RAAWWWWWWWWWWWWWRRRRRRRRRRRRRRRRRRR!!!!'

No sooner had the two *Rajasaurus* made a lightning dash towards the river than Padma and the others ran in the opposite direction. Padma and Labhuben held on to each other tightly on Bluethingosaurus's back. Rock Uncle held on to his bag as they sped away, unable to capture the wild chase with his camera.

Huffing and panting, the *Rajasaurus* duo stood in the shallow waters of the Narmada seaway, but there was no one in sight. They soon realized that they had been tricked and turned around quickly. They saw Mahaan and Baahu and the rest of them speeding away swiftly into the distance.

'Oh dear! They've seen us!' Mahaan said to the others as he turned around to see if they were safe. 'And they're after us!'

The plan hadn't worked after all. The *Rajasaurus* were faster than Rock Uncle had imagined. The giant strides of the *Titanosaurus* were no match for the ferocity of the *Rajasaurus*.

Then suddenly, the *Rajasaurus* were no longer in hot pursuit. They had spotted some other *Rajasaurus* feasting on fresh prey and turned around to join them. But Bluethingosaurus, Mahaan and Baahu continued full-speed till they could no longer hear the royal *Rajasaurus*.

'This is unbelievable! We escaped the royal prince of the Narmada, the *Rajasaurus narmadensis*! King Jabalpuriya will be mighty pleased to learn about it,' said Rock Uncle, while Baahu and Mahaan looked like they were still reeling from what they

had just gone through.

'Rock Uncle, you can now add one more characteristic to your study of the *Rajasaurus* – they are lazy dinosaurs!' said Padma.

'You bet!' replied Rock Uncle. 'They gave up a feast of *Titanosaurus* for a ready meal!

'Well, I won't lie. After a long day's work, I wouldn't mind if someone served me a ready meal too!' added Labhuben, as everyone chuckled and laughed.

They were all relieved that the nightmare was over. The Narmada looked calm and peaceful, oblivious of the happenings along the river bank.

A New Dawn

The weather was getting warmer. Padma and Labhuben got off Bluethingosaurus's back. They held hands and sat down by the banks of the Narmada like two friends – talking, giggling and dipping their toes in its cool waters.

'If we can't find your family, we will take you back with us to Jabalpuriya,' said Mahaan to Bluethingosaurus. 'You can stay with us.' Both Baahu and Mahaan had become quite fond of Bluethingosaurus. They wanted to do whatever it took to find his family but were willing to take him home if they failed in their quest.

Rock Uncle was busy taking pictures. He often tried to zoom in to get a better shot. On one occasion, when he was zooming in on a scene, he saw a few dinosaurs looking down at something. When he looked more carefully, he

realized that they were all blue. Rock Uncle jumped up and did a little jig!

'Blue dinosaurs! Blue *Isisaurus*! I just spotted some at a distance! We must have reached the Dongargaon hill in Chandrapur, Maharashtra!' announced Rock Uncle, as he showed everyone the pictures he had just shot.

Without wasting any time, they galloped like stallions in the direction in which Rock Uncle was pointing, until they reached the site where the blue dinosaurs had been seen. There were small and large Bluethingosauruses. They had finally found Bluethingosaurus's home!

Is this the end of our search? Padma thought.

But the atmosphere there was gloomy.

'What happened? Is something wrong? Can we help you?' Baahu asked a crying *Isisaurus*.

'There were four eggs in this pit. But only three hatched. The fourth egg is missing,' said the *Isisaurus*, with tears in her eyes. 'My baby! I hope the vicious *Rajasaurus* did not gobble it up. We have lost so many family members to the carnivores.'

Bluethingosaurus then emerged from behind Mahaan and Baahu. For the first time in his life, he saw someone else who looked just like him. He instantly recognized his mother among all those gathered there! He ran towards her, hugging and nuzzling her, delighted to have finally found his mother.

'I found me mummmmmyyy! Me mummmmmyyy! I say thaaaaaaaaaank youuuuuuuuuu aaaalllll!' Bluethingosaurus squealed with delight.

Rock Uncle asked everyone to pose for a picture – and when he found that they were not fitting in one frame, he climbed a nearby tree and took a picture from the top.

Celebrations ensued in Chandrapur. Padma, Labhuben and Rock Uncle cooked a feast for everyone, just like they had done in Jabalpuriya. Everyone feasted on the good food. Broken tree stubs and branches turned into drums, and a fistful of seeds were used as maracas. The humans witnessed a joyful dinosaur dance, unlike anything they had seen before! The dinosaurs formed a circle around Bluethingosaurus and his mother, and performed a strange dance ritual – taking two steps forward, and one step back, they shook their tails and nodded their heads. This enjoyable performance continued for a while.

'Maybe some of our dance forms are modified versions of the dinosaur dance!' said Padma, as she, Labhuben, Rock Uncle, Mahaan and Baahu joined in.

Music and mirth filled the air.

The humans stayed there for the night at the behest of the *Isisaurus* family. The blue dinosaurs made tent-like structures from huge palm leaves for them to sleep in. Rock Uncle, Labhuben and Padma thanked Bluethingosaurus's family for their hospitality. Padma hugged Bluethingosaurus and wished him goodnight.

'A roof after so many days!' said Padma.

'And to sleep without the fear of being attacked!' said Labhuben.

Mahaan and Baahu did not stay back. Their job was done. They had obeyed and fulfilled the King's orders, and now, it was time to head back to Jabalpuriya. The *Isisaurus* family showed them a route where they would not have to encounter the ferocious *Rajasaurus narmadensis*.

Rock Uncle gave the glowing rock back to Mahaan and Baahu along with a thank you note for the King. They were all so grateful to the King of Jabalpuriya. He also gave Padma the jar with the dinosaur egg that he had kept safely in his bag.

'My precious dinosaur egg!' said Padma as she removed the egg carefully from the jar. She ran her fingers along the egg – she loved feeling the rough lines on its surface. It was intact despite the long journey it had undertaken along the Narmada. She gently placed the egg back into the jar and screwed on the lid again.

The countless stars in the sky ushered the night in. The moon shone bright. Padma could even see the crater formations on the moon's pearly white surface. It almost seemed to be keeping guard, its light falling directly on the dinosaur egg. Padma had a faint memory of something, but she couldn't quite tell what it was. Somehow this felt so similar to their last night back home.

Everyone in Chandrapur was asleep.

The next morning, the rooster crowed, the sparrows chirped and the canaries sang a melodious song.

'Padma, wake up!' When Padma opened her eyes, Labhuben was staring down at her. Padma looked around. She saw the familiar roof and walls of her house. The jar lay on the shelf like she had kept it the night before they time-travelled into the Cretaceous Period. They seemed to have returned to the 21st century.

Padma ran to look out of the window. She saw fields of cotton swaying in the breeze.

'How did we come back home? Or did the house come back to us?' Padma asked Labhuben. 'Was it the moon? It was shining bright on both the nights! The egg! It has come back with us! I don't know what's inside it, but I'm sure it's not an ordinary dinosaur egg!'

Labhuben looked perplexed. 'What are you mumbling about, Padu? The egg is exactly where you put it last night – in the jar. Look.'

Padma fell silent. Did Baa not remember their adventure?

'Baa, don't you remember Bluethingosaurus? Don't you remember our adventure along the Narmada with Rock Uncle, Mahaan, Baahu and my Bluethingo?'

'Blue— what?' Labhuben said, laughing curiously. 'Are you talking about one of your drawings? Such an odd name!'

It was clear to Padma that Labhuben had no recollection of their crazy adventure in the Cretaceous Period. Padma rushed out to look for Rock Uncle. Maybe he would remember! And the camera – they had pictures! Seeing her take off at such speed, Labhuben followed.

At the flatland, the cows were grazing happily. But there was chaos everywhere. People huddled together in groups. They spotted Rock Uncle with Pranavbhai, a local farmer.

'Dinkarbhai!' Pranavbhai exclaimed. 'Someone stole rocks from here in the quiet of the night! Look, they are all gone!'

Rock Uncle looked alarmed. So did Padma and Labhuben.

'These are no ordinary rocks! They are our national treasure – prehistoric fossils that were found here,' replied Rock Uncle, worriedly.

Padma moved closer to Rock Uncle. 'Do you have photos of Bluethingosaurus, Rock Uncle?' she asked with a growing sense of alarm.

'Blue … who?' Rock Uncle asked.

'Bluethingosaurus … our blue dinosaur friend from the …' Padma's voice trailed off.

She had realized by now that neither Rock Uncle nor her Baa recalled their time with Bluethingosaurus. Before she could press further, Rock Uncle had walked away to inspect the site from where the fossils had been stolen. He was anxious to find out who the trespassers were. 'We need to get to the bottom of this robbery. The scoundrels even took the rock with dinosaur eggs that Padma had discovered.'

Labhuben nodded in agreement.

'My Bluethingosaurus! How I shall miss him!' lamented Padma. Was she the only one who remembered the strange, blue creature that had surprised them by sticking its head out of the trees?

Labhuben's voice broke her train of thought.

'Time to go, Padu! Harrrrrrrrrrrrrrrrrrrrrrrrrrrrrrrrrrrrrrrrrrrrrrr Chk Chk Harrrrrrrrrrrrrrrrrrrrrrrrrrrrrrrr!'

Labhuben was ushering the cows out of the flatland. The herd of cows swayed in uniform motion. The sound of bells tied around their necks was like wind chimes tinkling together.

Padma glanced at the flatland before following Labhuben.

Nothing had changed. Yet every day was indeed different.

All About
Indian Dinosaurs

Contents

Introduction

Ihope your journey along the Narmada was as fascinating and exciting as Padma's adventure with Labhuben, Rock Uncle and the adorable Bluethingosaurus. But our adventure is not over yet.

Did you know that in the last three decades, Palaeontologists from India have discovered around 20-25 species of dinosaurs? Some of these are very significant as they help understand the evolution and extinction of dinosaurs.

India has a very rich fossil heritage of dinosaurs. The sedimentary-rich regions in the states of Madhya Pradesh, Gujarat, Maharashtra, Rajasthan, Meghalaya, Telangana, Andhra Pradesh and even parts of Jammu and Kashmir have thrown up some amazing surprises during excavations. And did you know that the first dinosaur fossil to be discovered in India was in 1828, only four years after the first dinosaur fossil ever was discovered in the world?

Padma's adventure along the Narmada would have given you a fair idea about the dinosaurs that lived in India. But there is more! Turn this page to enter the exclusive world of India's very own dinosaurs and the people behind their discoveries. And learn more about the fascinating creatures that lived in our country millions of years ago!

'Reasoning from analogy at Jubbulpore, where some of the basaltic cappings of the hills had evidently been thrown out of craters long after this surface had been raised above the waters, and become the habitation both of vegetable and animal life, I made the first discovery of fossil remains in the Nerbudda valley. I went first to a hill within sight of my house in 1828, and searched exactly between the plateau of basalt that covered it, and the stratum immediately below; and there I found several small trees with roots, trunks, and branches, all entire, and beautifully petrified. They had been only recently uncovered by the washing away of a part of the basaltic plateau. I soon after found some fossil bones of animals.'

—Major-General Sir William Henry Sleeman

(A soldier and administrator in the Bengal Army in British India, Sir W.H. Sleeman's long-term interest in natural history led him to the discovery of the first ever dinosaur fossil found in India, in 1828. It was in Jabalpur, along the Narmada River.)

This is how it all began...

How It All Began!

Welcome to the fascinating world of our very own dinosaurs. Dinosaurs that were the citizens of India about 66 million years ago.

Ever wondered why dinosaur fossils are found in most parts of the world? Or why the dinosaur fossils found in distant Africa or South America or Madagascar are so similar to the fossils found in India?

From Supercontinents to Present-day Continents

What are now called 'continents' were once supercontinents. About 270–300 million years ago, the Earth was one huuuuuumongousssssss land mass called Pangea. The word 'Pangea' comes from the Greek word 'pangaia', which means 'all the Earth'!

> **Did you know?**
>
> *A single large ocean called Panthalassa surrounded this single large land mass of pangaia.*

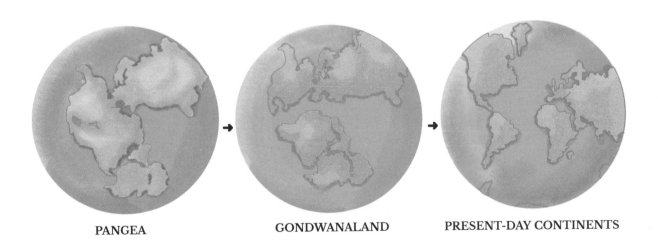

PANGEA   GONDWANALAND   PRESENT-DAY CONTINENTS

Fig. 1: From Pangea to present-day continents

Then, about 200 million years ago, the shifting of the Earth's tectonic plates—layers under the Earth's crust that move and cause earthquakes and volcanoes—broke Pangea down into two parts – Laurasia in the north (North America, Europe, Asia) and Gondwanaland in the south (South America, Indian subcontinent, Australia, Africa). This marks the beginning of the Triassic Period when dinosaurs evolved on Earth.

Another 150 million years later, Gondwanaland split further – into Africa and South America in the west and into India, Madagascar, Australia and Antarctica in the east. This is the Jurassic Period when the dinosaurs grew in numbers – both in terms of species and population. The dinosaurs that co-existed on one single land mass before, now roamed across different continents. This explains why similar skull and bone fossils are being discovered in different parts of the world even as we read this.

To give you an example, *Rajasaurus narmadensis* bears a distinct resemblance to its Madagascan counterpart, *Majungasaurus*, and to *Carnotaurus* from South America.

The Wonderful Narmada: Our Fossil-Rich Heritage

Call her Narmada. Call her Nerbudda. Call her Rewa. Or call her Namade, as did the Greek geographer Ptolemy in his scripts from second century AD. This ancient, historic and holy river that flows across the breadth of India is the fifth-largest river in India and the largest river in the state of Madhya Pradesh (MP). Originating from the Narmada Kund, a small reservoir in the mighty Amarkantak Hills of MP, it flows through the Vindhya and Satpura mountain ranges. It is over 1,300 km long and travels through the states of MP, Gujarat and Maharashtra.

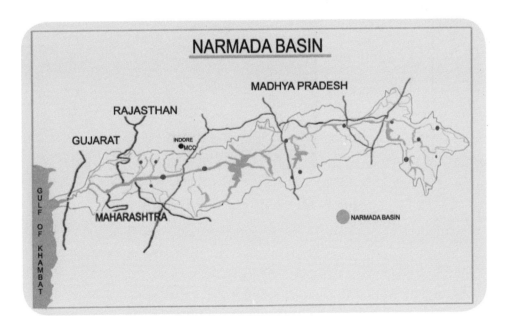

Fig. 2: The dinosaur trail along the Narmada river

What is the Lameta Formation?

You will come across the term 'Lameta Formation' many times while reading this book because it is the most fossil-rich region of India. The Lameta Formation is a multilayered sedimentary belt that runs along the banks of the Narmada. It was formed in the Upper Cretaceous Period (100.5 mya to 66 mya). The fossils are found buried in marble and dolomitic cliffs, which are covered with sedimentary rocks for a stretch of nearly 200 km. These sedimentary deposits have helped preserve the fossils for millions of years.

Fossils of popular dinosaurs from India, such as the *Titanosaurus*, *Indosaurus*, *Laevisuchus*, *Isisaurus* and *Jainosaurus*, have been unearthed here!

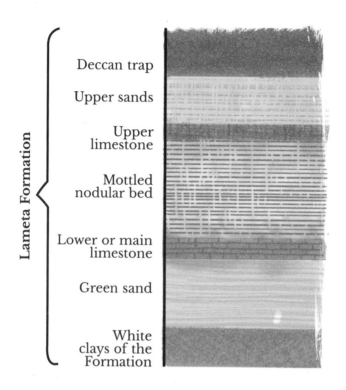

Fig. 3: The Lameta Formation

Other Fossil-Rich Regions

Have you heard of the Maleri, Dharmaram and Kota Formations?

These formations, too, are fossil-rich sedimentary belts. They are found in Andhra Pradesh, along the banks of the rivers Pranhita and Godavari. They are home to the dinosaur fossils from the Late Triassic Period (251 mya to 200 mya) and Early Jurassic Period (200 mya to 146 mya), such as *Alwalkeria maleriensis* and *Barapasaurus tagorei*.

A significant number of fossilized bones of sauropods have also been discovered in the sedimentary formation called Mahadek Formation at Dirang, a small village near Ranikor, West Khasi Hills district, Meghalaya. Similarly, some areas of Kutch and Rajasthan, too, are considered fossil sites with high potential for discoveries.

Period-Wise Classification of Dinosaurs Found in India

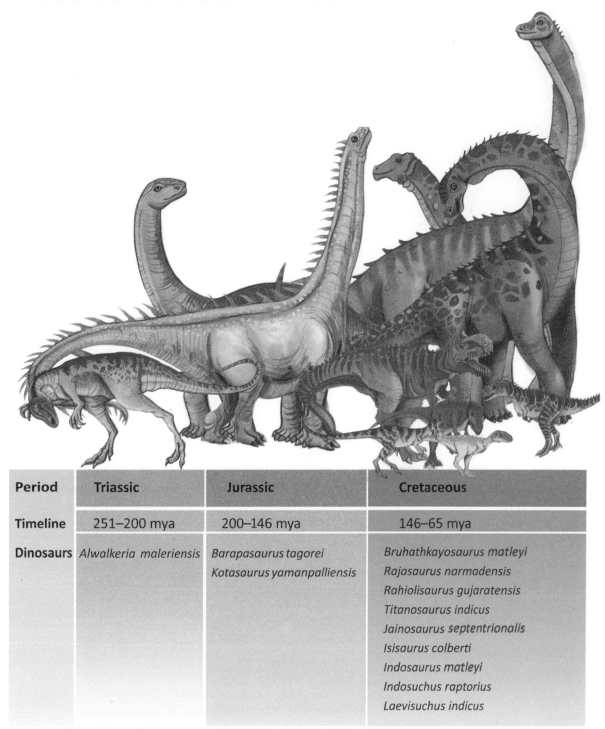

Period	Triassic	Jurassic	Cretaceous
Timeline	251–200 mya	200–146 mya	146–65 mya
Dinosaurs	*Alwalkeria maleriensis*	*Barapasaurus tagorei* *Kotasaurus yamanpalliensis*	*Bruhathkayosaurus matleyi* *Rajasaurus narmadensis* *Rahiolisaurus gujaratensis* *Titanosaurus indicus* *Jainosaurus septentrionalis* *Isisaurus colberti* *Indosaurus matleyi* *Indosuchus raptorius* *Laevisuchus indicus*

Note: *mya:* million years ago; *myo:* million years old

Fossil Sites and Hatcheries in India

Would you like to see and hold dinosaur fossils? Well, if you're anywhere in India, they're perhaps not too far from where you are!

I get wide-eyed, astonished looks from most people when I tell them that India has some of the world's largest fossil excavation sites and hatcheries! Of late, thanks to social media, people are becoming more and more aware about them. Still, most people are in the dark about where these sites are and what they contain.

Rahioli in Gujarat is the third-largest fossil excavation site and the second-largest hatchery in the world. (The other major nesting sites are in Aix-en-Provence in France and in Mongolia.) Located 70 km from Ahmedabad, Rahioli is home to the dinosaurs from the Cretaceous Period.

Another fossil excavation site is in Telangana, near Kota village. Dinosaur fossils from the Jurassic Period were discovered here.

↑ **Fig. 4: Entrance to the Rahioli Dinosaur Park, Kheda, Gujarat**
Picture courtesy: Aatish Shroff

Fig. 5: Plate V, Dinosaur Fossil Park, established by the Geological Survey of India in 1983, in Balasinor-Rahioli Area, Kheda, Gujarat
Picture Courtesy: *Dinosaurs of India*, Ashok Sahni, National Book Trust, India

What are Nesting Sites or Hatcheries?

Dinosaur nesting sites are places where dinosaurs made pits in the ground and laid eggs. However, these pits got buried under sand and rocks when a series of natural calamities—volcanic eruptions, earthquakes, tsunamis—took place in different parts of the world.

The buried eggs were fossilized and are now being discovered during excavations. It is important to remember that finding fossilized eggs is an incredibly rare thing. Padma was a lucky girl!

Hold your breath! The largest Cretaceous site in the world is in central India and it extends from Kutch in the west to Nagpur in the east, then up to north of Hyderabad (Adilabad) and further down to Tamil Nadu. In all, it covers a whopping 10,000 sq. km! Phew!

Fig. 6: Plate XXII, nest of a Theropod from dinosaur park,
Rahioli, shows eggs of elongated shapes

Picture Courtesy: *Dinosaurs of India*, Ashok Sahni, National Book Trust, India

Whose Egg is This?

You can tell which dinosaur the egg fossil belongs to by looking at its shape.

1. *Megaloolithus* eggs: As the name suggests, these are 'large eggs', about 16 cm in diameter. They typically belong to sauropods.
2. *Elongatoolithus* eggs: These are elongated eggs and typically belong to theropods.
3. *Ornithischian* eggs: These are very tiny and belong to small dinosaurs.

Fun with Nomenclature

Did you ever wonder why most dinosaur names end with a 'saurus' or why they have such absurd names?

To start with, two Greek words, *deinos* (meaning terrible) and *sauros* (meaning lizard) were used to create the word Dinosaur!

But how do they get such strange-sounding, tongue-twisting names?

Typically, dinosaur names are indicative of their distinct physical features, their place of discovery, the name of the Palaeontologist who discovered them or the scientist who first described them in a research paper! They are a combination of two Greek or two Latin words, or one Greek and one Latin word, in the following order:

Genus + species

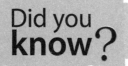 *Every dinosaur name must be approved by the International Commission on Zoological Nomenclature.*

Also, most popular dinosaur names end in 'saurus' or 'suchus' or 'raptor'. While sauros means 'lizard' in Greek, suchus means 'crocodile' (derived from the word 'soukhos', an Egyptian crocodile god) and raptor means a 'bird of prey' in Latin.

Don't forget to italicize the genus and species names. It's a rule!

Among the dinosaurs found in India, *Alwalkeria maleriensis* was named after the British Palaeontologist Alick Walker. His name forms the genus name of the dinosaur, while its species name comes from the Maleri Formation in Andhra Pradesh, where it was discovered. *Bruhathkayosaurus* means a huge-bodied lizard ('bruhath' means 'huge' and 'kaya' means 'body' in Sanskrit).

If you were a Palaeontologist, and you discovered a new dinosaur fossil, what would you name it?

Excavation! Expedition! Excitement!

Isn't that a cool tongue-twister? But you know what is cooler? Finding your own dinosaur fossil bone!

But how do you go about doing that?

It's not very easy to discover and identify a dinosaur fossil bone. But once you know the trick, it's not that difficult either. And it is very interesting!

The Cool Tools

Before you set out to dig up a fossil, let's look at all the cool tools you will need to pack for your expedition.

1. **Maps** that show you where fossils are likely to be accessible for excavation

Fig. 7: Typical contents of a Palaeontologist's tool kit

(topographical maps) and maps that show the rock types and their age (geologic maps). It is best to look for fossils in places where the rocks are 250 to 65 million years old and in areas that are not covered with dense vegetation. Deserts and rocky areas are easier sites for excavation.

2. **Brushes** to remove the loose dust and dirt on the specimen.

3. **Shovels, rock hammers, awls** and **chisels** to remove the rocks covering the fossil fragment. Once you get closer to the specimen, you will need smaller and finer knives.

4. **Special glue** to keep the bone intact.

5. **Plaster** and **burlap** to create 'field jackets' around the specimens so you can carry them to the lab safely.

Don't forget to carry food, plenty of water and sunblock as most fossil sites are in hot, dry and arid regions.

From Discovery to Collection

1. **Prospecting:** You need to travel and hike slowly across ridges and rocky terrain for many miles. Don't take your eyes off the ground and keep looking for fossil fragments on the surface.

2. **Identifying:** Generally, identification of fossil bones is based on what you find – teeth, bone, egg. Once you discover a fossil, you need to first compare it to existing discoveries by checking reference books, or records at labs, universities and natural history museums. If you find a record of a specimen with the same features as your specimen, it is an already discovered species. The best part is when there is no record of what you have found! Guess what? You've probably discovered an entirely new dinosaur species!

3. **Brushing:** You need to remove the loose dirt from the surface to see the specimen clearly to check if there's more than just one fossil fragment.

4. **Quarrying:** Once you are sure there's a fossil fragment at a specific spot, the real work starts. You chisel the rocks to get closer to the fossil. Once you see the fossil clearly, apply glue in the cracks so the bone does not fall apart.

5. **Digging a trench:** After you secure the fossil bone, you need to dig a trench

Fig. 8: A Palaeontologist excavating at a fossil site

around it in a way that it is still encased in the surrounding rock. Such a rock is called a 'matrix'.

6. **Plastering:** The bone should now be covered with a plaster, like bone fracture casts, to keep it safe. It's a very precious, fragile thing!

7. **Shipping:** As the cast hardens, the specimen is snapped away from the rock and carried to its destination safely. Depending on its size and weight, you might even need a truck to do so.

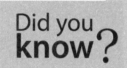 *There are people who use dental tools, mini grinding wheels, miniature jackhammers and tiny sand blasters to extract the fossil from the plaster jacket and surrounding rock. They are called 'fossil preparators'. How exciting!*

Once extracted, the specimen is observed through a high-precision microscope to check if all the features are intact. Special adhesives and glues are used to conserve the specimen. Finally, the discovery is officially recorded.

So, are you ready for some excavation expedition excitement?

Cool Trivia from a Real Excavation Expedition!

During the excavation of the *Rajasaurus* in Rahioli, Gujarat, many villagers sat alongside Palaeontologist Suresh Srivastava all day – trying to make sense of what was going on. Finally, unable to contain their curiosity, they asked him what was really happening. When Suresh Srivastava replied that he was digging up fossilized dinosaur bones, they did not believe him. Instead, they were convinced that the Palaeontologist was trying to unearth the golden chariot that belonged to a demon killed by Lord Krishna at that spot! Amused by their response, Suresh Srivastava told them that he would give them a wheel if he found one.

Up Close and Personal with Our Dinosaurs

Alwalkeria maleriensis

You can call the *Alwalkeria* the father of all dinosaurs found in India, because it is the earliest dinosaur to have roamed India (nearly 250–200 million years ago in the Triassic Period). It was discovered in the Maleri Formation, Andhra Pradesh.

Originally, in 1987, it was named *Walkeria* by Palaeontologist Sankar Chatterjee in honour of the British Palaeontologist, Alick Walker. However, since the genus name was already taken by another species, they changed it to *Alwalkeria*. The species name, *maleriensis*, comes from the Maleri Formation where it was found.

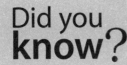 **Did you know?** *These dinosaurs could be hiding under your bed, and you wouldn't even know. Yes, they were really, really small and slender compared to the popular dinosaurs we know of! They weighed 2–3 kg and were only about 1.5 m in length!*

The *Alwalkeria* is known only from a few jaw bones and incomplete vertebrae. But from their sharp teeth, the Palaeontologists could tell that they were athletic predators that preyed on smaller vertebrates and plant life.

Fig. 9: *Alwalkeria maleriensis* a dinosaur from the Triassic Period

Barapasaurus tagorei

Have you heard of Pochampally sarees or Pochampally Ikat silk? Chances are that your mother would have! One of the most ancient weaving villages in the world, Pochampally is a village in Telangana, South India. Known as the Silk City of India, it is also a world heritage site as part of the 'iconic saree-weaving clusters of India'.

However, what most people do not know is that it's also a very rich fossil excavation site. Fossils of the *Barapasaurus tagorei*, from the Jurassic Period (199.6–145.5 million years old), were discovered in Pochampally, near the Kota formation that runs along the Pranhita–Godavari basins by Palaeontologists Sohan Lal Jain, Tharavat S. Kutty, Tapan Roy Chowdhury and Sankar Chatterjee in 1959. But it was documented only many years later in 1975.

The name *Barapasaurus* means 'big-legged lizard' ('bara' means 'huge' and 'pa' means 'legs' in Bengali, and 'sauros' means lizard in Greek). The species name *tagorei* is in honour of the Indian Nobel Laureate and poet par excellence Rabindranath Tagore.

Fig. 10: *Barapasaurus tagorei*

A herbivorous quadrupedal sauropod, *Barapasaurus tagorei* is estimated to be about 15 m long and weighing a few tonnes. Its skeleton is mounted in an exhibit at the Museum of Palaeontology, Indian Statistical Institute, Kolkata.

Fig. 11: Mounted *Barapasaurus tagorei* skeleton at the Geological Studies Unit (GSU) Museum

Picture courtesy: Indian Statistical Institute and Geological Studies Unit

Kotasaurus yamanpalliensis

Do you like doing dinosaur jigsaw puzzles? But what if the 840 jigsaw puzzle pieces (bones) belonged to 12 individual dinosaurs of the same species? And to complicate things further, imagine the head was missing!

That's the *Kotasaurus yamanpalliensis*, one of the most primitive sauropods (from the Early Jurassic Period, 200–145 million years ago) to have been discovered anywhere in the world!

The *Kotasaurus yamanpalliensis* was discovered by Late Dr Yadagiri in 1988 in the Kota Formation (thus, *Kotasaurus*) near the village of Yamanapalli (reflected in the word *yamanpalliensis*) in the district of Adilabad, Telangana. Standing about 9 m tall and weighing roughly 2.5 tonnes, this quadrupedal herbivore was assembled from 840 bones belonging to 12 different individual *Kotasaurus*!

Fig. 12: *Kotasaurus yamanpalliensis*

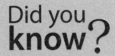
In 2000, the Geological Survey of India (GSI) mounted and installed a composite and complete skeleton—85 per cent of which was actual fossil bones—of the *Kotasaurus* at the Dinosaurium in the Birla Science Centre, Hyderabad.

Fig. 13: Mounted *Kotasaurus yamanpalliensis* skeleton at the Dinosaurium, Birla Science Centre, Hyderabad

Picture courtesy: GSI Images

Bruhathkayosaurus matleyi

Dinosaur size estimations are always controversial and heavily debated. Perhaps no two studies can give the exact same dimensions for the same dinosaur. One of the biggest debates around this has been: which is the largest dinosaur to have ever lived?

Bruhathkayosaurus matleyi ('bruhath' meaning 'large', 'kayo' meaning 'body', 'saurus' meaning 'lizard') means a 'large-bodied lizard'. And it has been part of this debate.

According to a paper published by Late Dr Yadagiri and Ayyasami in 1989, the shin bone of a *Bruhathkayosaurus* was estimated to be 29 per cent larger than that of an *Argentinosaurus*. Some Palaeontologists also say that it weighed more than 100 tonnes!

Unfortunately, there is not enough evidence as the specimens are feared to have been washed away in a tsunami. So, no concrete claims can be made to establish *Bruhathkayosaurus* as perhaps the largest dinosaur to have walked this planet.

Fig. 14: *Bruhathkayosaurus matleyi*

Titanosaurus indicus

The giants of Jabalpuriya, Mahaan and Baahu, are Titanosaurs belonging to the Late Cretaceous Period. The name literally means 'Titanic Lizards', from the mythical Titans of Ancient Greece.

These herbivorous sauropods, nearly 30–40 feet long and weighing close to 12 tonnes, were officially named 50 years after they were first discovered in 1828. But the specimens got lost and were discovered again 184 years after they were first found! **How bizarre!**

1828: Lieutenant Colonel William Henry Sleeman discovered it at the Lameta Formation of the Bara Simla and Chhota Simla region of Jabalpur, Madhya Pradesh.

1877: Richard Lydekker, an English naturalist, geologist and writer named it *Titanosaurus indicus*.

Fig. 15: *Titanosaurus indicus*

However, the specimens went missing after they were sent to the Natural History Museum in London for preservation!

The *Titanosaurus* Rediscovered in a Cupboard. Really?

Palaeontologists Dhananjay Mohabey and Subhasis Sen found one of the main specimens in 2012 in a cupboard in the GSI Headquarters, Kolkata. It was part of Lydekker's collection of Mesozoic vertebrate fossils. It was rediscovered 135 years after it was named!

Can you imagine ...

The rest of the specimen's plaster casts were found in the GSI museums of Nagpur, Jaipur and Gandhinagar by Dhananjay Mohabey and Jeffrey Wilson of the University of Michigan under a joint collaborative effort.

The originals are still somewhere in the British Natural History Museum. Does that make the *Titanosaurus indicus* the Kohinoor of Indian dinosaurs?

The Indian Abelisaurids

In 1933, Charles Alfred Matley discovered fossilized bones of bipedal carnivores that were described by Friedrich von Huene and Matley as theropods. These were later renamed as *Abelisauridae*. These theropods had stocky hindlimbs and short forelimbs with immobile elbow joints. They were found near Jabalpur from the Lameta Formation.

The *Abelisauridae* family includes:

- *Indosuchus raptorius* (pronounced: Indo–sew–kes): 'Indo' meaning 'Indus' and 'suchus' derived from 'soukhos', the Egyptian crocodile god.

- *Indosaurus matleyi* (pronounced: Indo–saw–ras): Meaning the 'Indian Lizard'.

- *Laevisuchus indicus* (pronounced: Lay–we–sew–kes): 'Laevis' means 'light' in Latin, which makes it the 'Light Indian Lizard'.

Fig 16: The Abelisaurids

- *Rahiolisaurus gujaratensis* (pronounced: Rai–yoli–saw–ras): Literally meaning 'the dinosaur discovered from Rahioli, Gujarat'.

Abelisauridae (Abel's Lizards, named after Argentinian Palaeontologist Roberto Abel) are carnivorous dinosaurs found in the Cretaceous Period (70–66 myo) from the supercontinent of Gondwanaland, which included Africa, South America, India and Madagascar.

While the *Indosaurus* and *Laevisuchus* were much smaller and lighter, the *Indosuchus* was relatively much larger (though smaller than the *Rajasaurus*), so it preyed on sauropods like the *Titanosaurus* and the *Isisaurus*.

Rajasaurus, too, is an abelisaurid, but we shall talk more about this princely dinosaur in a different chapter.

Rajasaurus narmadensis

The 65 million year old *Rajasaurus narmadensis*, an abelisaurid theropod, was discovered by Palaeontologist Suresh Srivastava from Jaipur GSI in 1983, from the fossil graveyard at Rahioli, in the Kheda district of Gujarat. This region is close to the statc highway and is called the Temple Hill.

The *Rajasaurus* sports a peculiar crest on its head, much like a crown. Hence the name *Rajasaurus*, which means 'Royal Lizard'. The word *narmadensis* stands for the sediment-rich Narmada river belt where it was discovered. A bipedal carnivore, it is about 9 m long with a very robust built, and a strong skull and neck.

The most fascinating part of the discovery was that he found a completely intact braincase just 3.5 m away from the backbones. He meticulously cleaned them. Near *Rajasaurus's* fossil bones, he discovered the fossil bones of individual sauropods, which meant that the *Rajasaurus* preyed on mighty sauropods like Mahaan and Baahu.

Fig. 17: *Rajasaurus narmadensis*

In 2001, two renowned Palaeontologists—Paul Sereno and Jeff Wilson—visited India and saw the *Rajasaurus's* bones sprawled across the GSI office floor. Together with experts at GSI, including Dr Ashok Sahni and Suresh Srivastava, they reconstructed this new species of dinosaurs and the *Rajasaurus* was ready to greet the world in 2003.

Fig. 18: Representation of the *Rajasaurus* braincase
Inspired by https://paulsereno.uchicago.edu/exhibits_casts/indian_dinosaurs/rajasaurus/

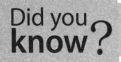 *Palaeontologist Suresh Srivastava has drawn a detailed map to show the position of every fossil bone as it lay in the field.*

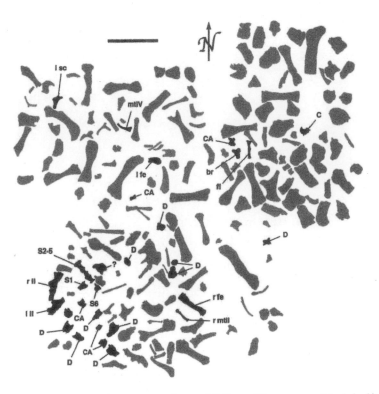

Fig. 19: Quarry map of the Temple Hill locality near Rahioli, Gujarat. Bones in black are the specimens of *Rajasaurus narmadensis* and grey, shaded bones belong to *Titanosaurian sauropods*.

Picture courtesy: Suresh Srivastava

'The roof of the skull has a raised lip, an indication of a horn ... There is nothing else in the world like this.'

—Jeff Wilson, renowned Palaeontologist

The *Rahiolisaurus gujaratensis* is another large-bodied abelisaurid theropod discovered in Rahioli. Although it resembles the *Rajasaurus*, it has much slender limbs.

Isisaurus colberti

Our very own *Bluethingosaurus*! Yes, it's an *Isisaurus colberti*. *Isisaurus* means 'ISI lizard', which comes from the initials of the Indian Statistical Institute (ISI) and 'saurus', meaning lizard. The species name '*colberti*' honours Edwin Harris Colbert, a noted American Palaeontologist.

Nearly 77–60 million years old, the *Isisaurus*, a sauropod from the Late Cretaceous Period, was discovered near the Dongargaon Hill in the Chandrapur district of Maharashtra in 1997 by Palaeontologists Sohan Lal Jain and Saswati Bandyopadhyay. It is one of the more complete skeletons to have been found, missing only the skull and a few limb bones.

Though they initially classified it as a *Titanosaur*, it was put in its own genus by Wilson and Upchurch in 2003. Thus, *Isisaurus* was born!

Fig. 20: *Isisaurus colberti*

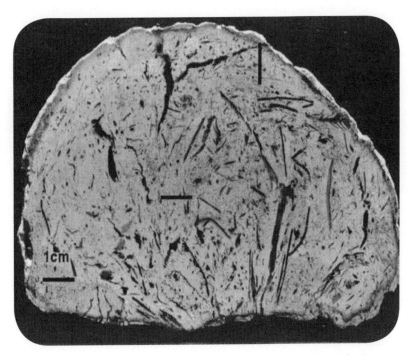

Fig. 21: Plate XXVI, coprolites with embedded and digested plant material

Picture courtesy: *Dinosaurs of India*, Ashok Sahni, National Book Trust, India

Can you imagine that one of the most important fossil remains of the *Isisaurus* was a coprolite (dinosaur poop) sprinkled with fungus?

The *Isisaurus* is the largest of all known Indian dinosaurs with a length of over 25 m and height of about 15 m. One of the most peculiar looking dinosaurs, the *Isisaurus* has the head of a hyena and the body of a modern-day giraffe! Of course, we can't tell if the *Isisaurus* was blue, but it is wonderful to imagine these mysterious creatures as colourful.

What colour would you like your favourite dinosaur to be?

The Very Interesting Sanajeh Snake

Curious what a snake is doing in a book of dinosaurs? Read on. Snakes came into being around 98 million years ago, towards the end of the dinosaur era. The 67.5 million-year-old fossils of the *Sanajeh indicus* were discovered in the Lameta Formation near the Dholi Dungri village of Gujarat.

In Sanskrit, 'sanaj' means 'ancient' and 'jeh' means 'gape' (early snakes with a limited oral gape). *Indicus* is derived from 'sindhu', the Indus river, which means it was discovered in the Indian subcontinent.

The *Sanajeh* snake is estimated to be approximately 3.5 m long.

But this was no ordinary snake fossil. The fossilized remains of *Sanajeh indicus* were coiled around a sauropod dinosaur egg, next to a hatchling!

This indicates that snakes frequently visited nesting grounds to prey on hatchling sauropods.

← Fig. 22: A rare association of a dinosaur egg with a partial skeleton of the Sanajeh Snake at Dhori Dungri. The three rocks (big rock with the snake skeleton and the two eggs) are clutched together.

Picture courtesy: *Dinosaurs of Gujarat*, Geological Survey of India Special Publication No. 106, Compiled by C. Srikarni, Suresh Srivastava, D.M. Mohabey, Z.G. Ghevariya, U.B. Mathur and G.N. Dwivedi

Recent Discoveries

Looking for evidence? Ready to play detective? Or, Palaeontologist?

Footprints

Jaisalmer, the Golden City of Rajasthan, is not just famous for its sand dunes and beautiful forts and palaces. Footprints of two dinosaurs from the Jurassic Period were discovered recently at the Thaiat Scarp section near Thaiat village, east of Jaisalmer. Palaeontologists Ján Schlögl and Grzegorz Pieńkowski, along with D.K. Pandey from the Department of Palaeontology, University of Rajasthan, discovered these footprints after the 9th International Jurassic Congress hosted by the University of Rajasthan.

Who did they belong to? Big dinosaurs or small? Terrestrial or flying?

The smaller footprint, the *Grallator tenuis*, was about 5.5 cm in length. It belongs to a theropod. The other footprint, *Eubrontes cf. giganteus*, had only three toe imprints (thus referred

→

Fig 23: Field photographs and drawings showing chronological details of the two dinosaur footprints determined as *Eubrontes cf. giganteus* and *Grallator tenuis*

Picture courtesy: 'Dinosaur footprints from the Thaiat ridge and their palaeoenvironmental background, Jaisalmer Basin, Rajastan, India'

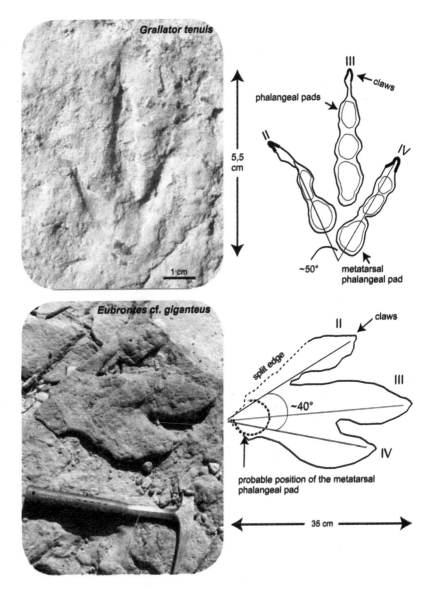

to as tridactyl) and was much larger at around 35.5 cm in length. It belongs to a bipedal theropod that is 5–6 m long.

Thus, footprints are an important discovery. Not only do they tell us more about the size of the animal, they also give information about whether the animal was walking or running, or if it walked alone or went about in herds.

The fossils of these dinosaurs have been found in the US, in Australia and in many countries across Europe. But their footprints have been found only in India. This is a very significant discovery in the history of Indian Palaeontology. And, more importantly, these footprints can tell us a lot about how the dinosaurs became extinct.

Sauropod Eggs

The 20th of January 2018 brought a flurry of activity and excitement at a site a few kilometres from Balasinor. Some local farmers had discovered a sauropod egg while carrying out their regular digging work. The egg is now with the GSI department.

← Fig. 23: The most recent discovery of a sauropod egg in Balasinor, Kheda district, Gujarat

Picture courtesy: Aaliya Sultana Babi

kaboom!
Where are the Dinosaurs Now?

The dinosaurs were the longest surviving creatures on our planet. They ruled the Earth for more than 150 million years. (Our ancestors are only 6 million years old and the human race evolved only about 2 million years ago). However, 65 million years ago, a catastrophic event changed everything on planet Earth. Animal and plant life, land, and water bodies – everything underwent a complete transformation.

Asteroid Impact on the Earth

If you are a diehard dinosaur fan, chances are you know about the huge asteroid or meteor that struck the Earth at the Mexican peninsula of Yucatan 65 million years ago. Many scientists believe that it created a massive crater, which is now underwater and is 100–200 km wide!

But what happened next?

This meteor triggered natural calamities in all parts of the world – volcanic eruptions, earthquakes and tsunamis rocked the planet. As a result, carbon dioxide levels increased, temperatures soared and sea levels decreased further, all of which caused water bodies to dry up. With no water to drink or plants to eat, the Cretaceous dinosaurs couldn't survive. This marked the end of the dinosaur race and the end of nearly 65 per cent of other plant and animal life!

Volcanic Eruptions

Around the time dinosaurs became extinct, about 68–65 million years ago, the Earth witnessed the biggest volcanic eruptions in the Deccan belt of India, chiefly in the states of Madhya Pradesh, Uttar Pradesh, Gujarat, Rajasthan, Maharashtra, Andhra Pradesh and Karnataka.

The eruptions created mountain ranges with layers and layers of lava deposits. These cake-like structures are best seen in the Western Ghats – from Nashik, Mahabaleshwar and Panchgani in the south. These are known as the Deccan Traps.

What Happened after the Eruptions?

A huge black cloud of volcanic dust covered the sky, preventing sunlight from entering the Earth's atmosphere. Harmful gases released into the air, causing 'acid rain'. All this led to a high amount of pollution, and in a period of 2–3 million years, the dinosaurs and over half of other plant and animal life went extinct.

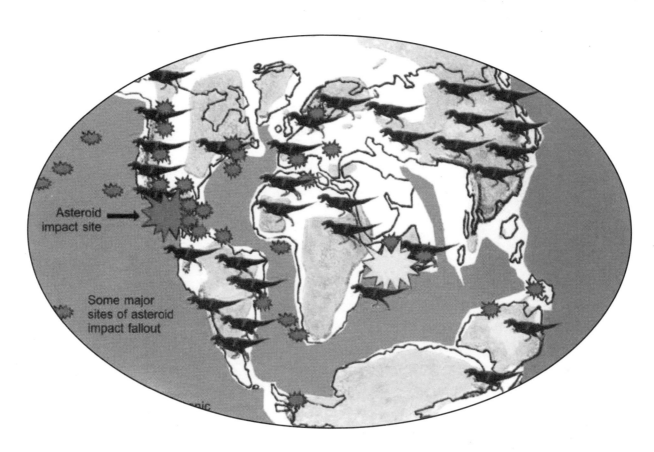

Fig. 24: Plate XXIII, extinction (asteroid and deccan volcanism)
Picture courtesy: *Dinosaurs of India*, Ashok Sahni, National Book Trust, India

Meet Aaliya: India's Amateur Palaeontologist and Dinosaur Enthusiast

From being the Princess of Balasinor to being an amateur Palaeontologist. Tell us more!

I am the youngest daughter of the Nawab Saheb of Balasinor and did my schooling from Sophia High School, Mount Abu.

Palaeontology was not something I had planned to pursue. The Palaeontologists and Geologists who we hosted at our palace invited me to accompany them to the fossil site. While initially it didn't spark any interest, gradually I found myself getting drawn towards the fossils. I am an English Literature student, and the study of fossils and geology was an alien subject to me. To add to this, there was not enough literature available at that time, especially about Indian dinosaurs. Tourists visited the site aimlessly as there was no knowledgeable professional to give them an educated tour of the place. With encouragement from friends, I decided to step in and bridge the gap between the tourists and the fossil site, and be a local guardian.

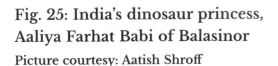

Fig. 25: India's dinosaur princess, Aaliya Farhat Babi of Balasinor
Picture courtesy: Aatish Shroff

93

What did you do to fuel your interest in learning more about Palaeontology?

I researched on the internet and every possible source. I wrote emails to my Palaeontologist friends seeking authentic details on discoveries made in India. I also watched shows on the National Geographic and Discovery channels and interacted with experts. I am, thus, a self-taught expert in this field.

Tell us more about your explorations in Balasinor and other fossil sites. How was it to find fossils in your backyard?

Whenever I have time, I go exploring in and around the fossil site and have discovered caches of eggs that were not known earlier. I have co-discovered a petroglyph, various fossils including tibia and femur bones, and parts of the spinal cord. I am extremely proud of my achievements over the last 20 years.

Today, the site is world famous, and we have people visiting from all over the country. It is the world's third-largest dinosaur fossil excavation site and the second-largest hatchery. When you visit, you see 72 acres of fenced area where you get to see the petrified remains of prehistoric life in its natural form.

Have you worked closely with other senior Palaeontologists?

India boasts of highly knowledgeable and senior Palaeontologists, and I've had the honour of interacting with and learning from the likes of Dr Ashok Sahni, Suresh Srivastava, Dr Dhananjay Mohabey and Srikarni. While in the US, I visited the University of Michigan at Ann Arbor, where Dr Jeff Wilson teaches. I was fortunate to attend a special class on dinosaurs in which he also mentioned our very own dinosaur site (Rahioli) and the *Rajasauraus*. I also visited the lab where the *Rajasauraus* and *Sanajeh indicus* were studied and prepared. I met experts who helped clean the petrified fossils and then visited Dr Paul Sereno's lab at the University of Chicago, where I met Tyler Keillor, a paleo-artist who prepared the models of both *Rajasauraus* and *Sanajeh indicus*. These were gifted to India, and are now in the Kolkata museum and the GSI office at Nagpur.

Is it true that we have a home-grown Jurassic Park in Gujarat?

I would rather call it the Cretaceous Park, as the dinosaurs found here are from the Late Cretaceous Period – not the Jurassic age, but I guess we are more familiar with the word 'Jurassic' because of the movie!

Any advice for aspiring Palaeontologists?

Palaeontology is not the study of dinosaurs alone but of every form of prehistoric life that existed. It's an amazing feeling to discover something that no one in this world knows about! Stay curious and read up a lot on recent discoveries from press releases and trusted websites like the GSI or National Geographic.

Good luck!

Do You Want to Be a Palaeontologist Too?

Palaeontology helps us bridge the gap between us and what happened in the universe millions and millions of years ago. They discover fossilized forms of prehistoric life, examine and study them, and present the findings to the world.

Palaeontology is an amalgamation of biology, geology and archaeology.

So, what does it take to be a Palaeontologist?

Curious minds discover. Curious minds want to learn more than they already know. Palaeontologists are such people! If you want to be a Palaeontologist, you need to be thirsty for knowledge and hungry for adventure.

> 'Curiosity is the forerunner of discovery.'
> —Richard Duke

If you want to study to be a Palaeontologist in India, it is recommended that you do a graduation programme in general sciences, with Biology and Geology as major subjects. You can then study further and do a post-graduation with 'Palaeobiology' as your research paper or major, depending on how the course is

> 'I have no special talents. I am only passionately curious.'
> —Albert Einstein

➡
Fig. 26: Author's son sitting by a nest of embedded fossil eggs, Rahioli Fossil Park
Picture courtesy: Aatish Shroff

offered at the institution. There are many international institutions that offer both graduate and post-graduate degrees in Palaeontology. In India, you could do a Palaeontology Refresher Course from Geological Survey of India (GSI) Institute, Bandlaguda, Hyderabad.

There is so much that has already been discovered. According to a study by National Geographic, a new dinosaur species is discovered almost every two weeks, and even if we had the bones of every single dinosaur, we would always underestimate the actual number of dinosaur species. Clearly, most dinosaurs are yet to be discovered!

> *'Palaeontology's practical use could be in its ability to help people understand the earth's evolution, including periods when it underwent significant climate change. That's our best bet to address climate change.'*
>
> *—Dr Ashok Sahni, 'Father of Indian Palaeontology'*

Do you think you can excavate new sites? Do you think you can challenge the discoveries and studies that have already been made – with fresh hypotheses and theories? Do you think you're The One? What if the most amazing dinosaur fossil yet to be discovered is right under your feet? Qualified Palaeontologists are well-respected and much sought-after people. Becoming a Palaeontologist can open many other opportunities as well. You could be a scholar and academician, teaching niche subjects that no one else can. The possibilities are endless!

So, let's get digging!

AT A GLANCE

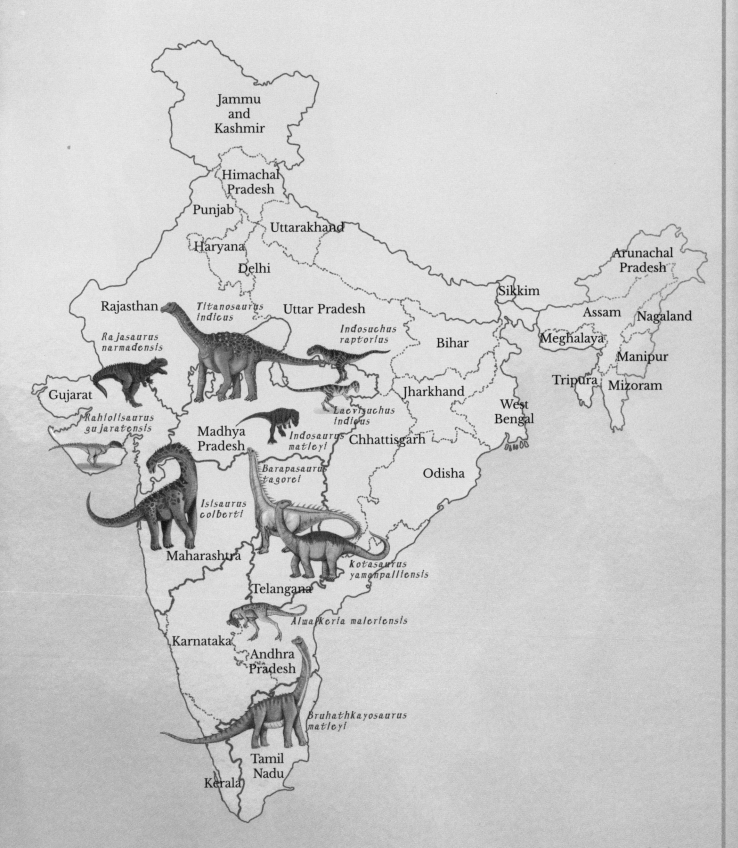

Map not to Scale

Jammu
and
Kashmir

Himachal
Pradesh

Punjab

Uttarakhand

Haryana

Delhi

Arunachal
Pradesh

Rajasthan

*Titanosaurus
indicus*

Uttar Pradesh

Sikkim

Assam

Nagaland

*Rajasaurus
narmadensis*

*Indosuchus
raptorius*

Bihar

Meghalaya

Manipur

Gujarat

Tripura

Mizoram

*Rahiolisaurus
gujaratensis*

*Laevisuchus
indicus*

Jharkhand

West
Bengal

Madhya
Pradesh

*Indosaurus
matleyi*

Chhattisgarh

*Barapasaurus
tagorei*

Odisha

*Isisaurus
colberti*

Maharashtra

*Kotasaurus
yamanpalliensis*

Telangana

Alwalkeria maleriensis

Karnataka

Andhra
Pradesh

*Bruhathkayosaurus
matleyi*

Tamil
Nadu

Kerala

Map not to Scale

Glossary

Acid rain: rain that has very harmful pollutants, causing damage to the environment and life

Bipedal: animals that use only two legs for walking

Composite: something that is composed or made up of several different elements

Decompose: decay or rotting of a dead body or organic matter

Dolomitic: white coloured rock made of dolomite (minerals of calcium magnesium carbonate)

Fossilized: organic matter preserved inside a rock for extremely long periods of time

Geology: study of geology, the science of earth and all the elements it is composed of

Metatarsals: the group of five bones that make a foot - they are long and give the foot its arch

Palaeobiology: study of the origin and evoluion of life (plants and animals) using fossilized specimens

Palaeontology: study of fossils of prehistoric and extinct plant and animal life

Phalangeal: related to phalanges (bones at the tips of fingers and toes)

Quadrupedal: four-footed animals

Quarry: a very big and deep pit from which rocks and stones have been removed

Sauropods: quadrupedal, herbivorous dinosaurs

Shin bone: the front part of the leg between the knee and the ankle

Specimen: an individual plant or animal used as an example for scientific study and research

Theropods: bipedal, carnivorous dinosaurs

Topography: natural and artificial features that define a particular area

Trench: a very long, narrow and deep ditch

Acknowledgements

Thank you, Arinjay and Vivikt, for loving dinosaurs so much that we almost involuntarily found ourselves going to the fossil site at Rahioli, Balasinor, where this story is set!

Suresh Srivastava Sir (just for this book – I'll call you Uncle when we speak), please accept my deepest gratitude. Not only for your invaluable inputs, encouragement and support for this book but also for getting me in touch with Ashok Sahni Sir.

Ashok Sahni Sir, I cannot tell you how grateful I am for your generosity and humility, your wisdom and counsel, and your precious insights and feedback that have been instrumental in shaping the non-fiction part of the book. Be it an email at 5 a.m. or at midnight, you've replied instantly from wherever you were. The world needs more people like you!

Aaliya, thank you for believing that I could do this book and giving me the confidence that you don't have to be a student of Palaeontology to write a book on dinosaurs!

Arinjay Shroff, Kruti Kothari Mody, Gauri Parab, Amrita Pai, Neepa Choksi and Sanyukta Paul, thank you so much for reading my story and putting up with my 52,826 questions on everything pertaining to the plot. Your honest feedback helped me improve the story and make it what it is today.

Suvidha, what would this book be without your stunning illustrations! It's almost like you stole the images from my mind and put them on paper with your genius!

Ateendriya, a heartfelt thank you for lending a fresh pair of eyes and your editorial expertise to the book and for putting it together!

Tina, this book would never have been possible without your vision. A super big thank you to you and HarperCollins India for giving me the opportunity to share the story of Padma and Bluethingosaurus's adventures with the world.

Children who are crazy about dinosaurs – thank you for inspiring me to write and stay crazy. Always! All you dinosaurs – this book and the hundreds of other books on dinosaurs would not exist without you. And to all of you reading this – thank you so much for picking up this book; I sincerely hope you enjoyed this adventure with us.

Vaishali Shroff

Further Reading

On Indian Dinosaurs:

1. Dr Sahni, Ashok. *Dinosaurs of India.* New Delhi: National Book Trust, 2016

2. Srivastava, Suresh et al. *Dinosaurs of Gujarat: A Compilation on the Various Dinosaur Fossil Finds and Related Life during Mesozoic Period in Gujarat, India.* Special Publication of the Geological Survey of India Series 106, 2017

3. Lal, Pranay. *Indica: A Deep Natural History of the Indian Subcontinent.* India: Penguin Random House, 2017

4. http://palaeontologicalsociety.in/

5. https://www.gsi.gov.in/webcenter/portal/

On Dinosaurs:

6. https://www.amnh.org/dinosaurs/

7. http://www.dinochecker.com/india.php

8. http://www.prehistoric-wildlife.com/

9. https://www.nationalgeographic.com/search/?q=dinosaurs

References

1. Pieńkowski G., Branski P., Pandey D.K., Schlögl J., Alberti M. and Fürsich M.T. 'Dinosaur Footprints from the Thaiat ridge and their palaeoenvironmental background, Jaisalmer Basin, Rajasthan, India.' *Volumina Jurassica* 13, no. 1 (2015): 17–26. Doi: 10.5604/17313708. 1148553

2. https://www.livescience.com/33460-how-dig-up-dinosaur.html

3. http://www.scholastic.com/browse/subarticle.jsp?id=21

4. https://www.britannica.com/place/Pangea

5. https://www.britannica.com/place/Narmada-River

6. https://telanganatoday.com/this-dinosaur-still-stands-tall

7. http://www.isical.ac.in/~gsu2008/index_files/About_us.htm

8. https://employee.gsi.gov.in/cs/idcplg?IdcService=DOC_INFO&dID=6672

Vaishali Shroff is hard to find at times. She's generally trapped inside one character or another, in one mysterious place or another. And when her strangely wired brain spews out characters and stories and there is nothing she can possibly do to hide them anymore, she writes. Her books include the multilingual, NCERT and CBSE recommended, *Raindrops* (longlisted for the Crossword Book Award 2013), *Ari* by Tulika Publishers, and *The Missing Bat* by Pratham Books. She represents India as an author for an Asia-wide reader series published by Oxford University Press, Asia Education. Her stories (both fiction and non-fiction), poetry, and articles have been featured in magazines, anthologies, school textbooks, and children's readers across leading publishing houses. *The Adventures of Padma and a Blue Dinosaur* is her first title with HarperCollins *Publishers* India. You can write to her at vaishali.shroff@gmail.com

Suvidha Mistry has studied Graphic Art. She has worked as a Graphic Head in several multimedia and advertising agencies. She has more than 30 illustrated books to her credit, having worked with many reputed publishing houses. A passionate photographer, she has conducted many workshops for children. Suvidha loves to experiment with pencils, Gouache and watercolours as well as application-based illustrations. She has been honoured by AWIC (Association of Writers and Illustrators for Children). She also participated in the Nambook010, International Children's Book Festival, Korea 2010. Her works have been exhibited in Korea and Bratislava.